The Unexplained
PHANTOMS AMONG US

Ghosts, Spirits, and Spectral Hauntings

by Spencer Brinker and Stuart Webb

Minneapolis, Minnesota

Credits
Cover and title page, © RDVector/Adobe Stock and © Vegorus/Adobe Stock and © Kooper/Adobe Stock; 4–5, © Marius Graf/Adobe Stock; 6, © tatui1761/Adobe Stock; 7, © iordani/Adobe Stock and © zalesky/Adobe Stock; 8, © William Maw Egley/Wikimedia; 9, © Kathy/Adobe Stock; 10–11, © EXTREME-PHOTOGRAPHER/iStock and © евгений ставников/Adobe Stock; 13, © Kathy/Adobe Stock and © JuliaTim/Adobe Stock and © ISO101/Adobe Stock; 13BR, © Public Domain/Wikimedia; 14BR, © Rear Admiral John W. Schmidt (Ret.)/Wikimedia; 14–15, © IG Digital Arts/Adobe Stock; 16–17, © muratart/Adobe Stock and © ffly/Adobe Stock; 17, © Kerim/Adobe Stock; 18–19, © Akarawut/Adobe Stock and © kimberrywood/Adobe Stock; 20–21, © Scott Griessel/Adobe Stock and © jinga80/Adobe Stock; 22–23, © Dr/Adobe Stock and © gitanna/Adobe Stock; 26–27, © mimadeo/Adobe Stock; 27TR, © Public Domain/Wikimedia; 27MR, © Public Domain/Wikimedia; 27BL, © Stevens, E. Winchester/National Library of Medicine; 28BL, © Himalayan Academy Publications/Wikimedia; 28–29, © GavinD/Getty Images; 30–31, © Mirrorpix/Getty Images; 32BL, © Colin/Wikimedia; 32–33, © Sung Kuk Kim/Adobe Stock; 33TR, © Sir John Everett Millais/Wikimedia; 33ML, © Public Domain/Wikimedia; 33MR, © Public Domain/Wikimedia; 33BL, © Public Domain/Wikimedia; 34, © Paul Delaroche/Wikimedia; 35, © Johnston, Frances Benjamin/Library of Congress; 36–37, © Mathieu LE MAUFF/iStock; 37T, © U.S. Federal prison/Wikimedia; 38TL, © C.T. Tatman/Wikimedia; 38BR, © Edmund Dulac/Wikimedia; 39, © Christophe Merceron/iStock; 41B, © Steve Snowden/Getty Images; 42–43, © DenisTangneyJr/iStock and © Apchanel/Adobe Stock and © sad/Adobe Stock; 43BL, © Public Domain/Wikimedia

Photo Illustrations by Kim Jones.

Bearport Publishing Company Product Development Team
Publisher: Jen Jenson; Director of Product Development: Spencer Brinker; Managing Editor: Allison Juda; Associate Editor: Naomi Reich; Associate Editor: Tiana Tran; Art Director: Colin O'Dea; Designer: Kim Jones; Designer: Kayla Eggert; Product Development Specialist: Owen Hamlin

Statement on Usage of Generative Artificial Intelligence
Bearport Publishing remains committed to publishing high-quality nonfiction books. Therefore, we restrict the use of generative AI to ensure accuracy of all text and visual components pertaining to a book's subject. See BearportPublishing.com for details.

Library of Congress Cataloging-in-Publication Data

Names: Webb, Stuart, author. | Brinker, Spencer, author.
Title: Phantoms among us : ghosts, spirits, and spectral hauntings / by Stuart Webb & Spencer Brinker.
Description: Minneapolis, Minnesota : Bearport Publishing Company, [2025] | Series: The unexplained | Includes bibliographical references and index. | Audience term: Children
Identifiers: LCCN 2024034555 (print) | LCCN 2024034556 (ebook) | ISBN 9798892328883 (library binding) | ISBN 9798892329187 (ebook)
Subjects: LCSH: Ghosts--Juvenile literature. | Spirits--Juvenile literature.
Classification: LCC BF1461 .W43 2025 (print) | LCC BF1461 (ebook) | DDC 133.1--dc23/eng/20240820
LC record available at https://lccn.loc.gov/2024034555
LC ebook record available at https://lccn.loc.gov/2024034556

© 2025 Arcturus Holdings Limited
This edition is published by arrangement with Arcturus Publishing Limited.

North American adaptations © 2025 Bearport Publishing Company. All rights reserved. No part of this publication may be reproduced in whole or in part, stored in any retrieval system, or transmitted in any form or by any means, electronic, mechanical, photocopying, recording, or otherwise, without written permission from the publisher.

For more information, write to Bearport Publishing, 5357 Penn Avenue South, Minneapolis, MN 55419.

Contents

A Ghostly World 4

Ancient Specters 6

Double (Spirit) Trouble 8

The Mysterious Ms. Sagée 12

Steer to the Nor'west! 14

Near to Death 18

Talking to the Dead 20

The Vennum Case 24

Did the Sisters Return? 28

The Bloody Tower 32

Lincoln's Ghost 34

Ghosts of Alcatraz 36

A Poet's Haunted House 38

Spirits "R" Us 40

Tombstone 42

Glossary 44

Read More 46

Learn More Online 46

Index 47

A Ghostly World

Throughout history and around the world, people have shared stories of encounters with ghosts and spirits. Is this widespread experience evidence of the survival of the soul after death? Or does it tell us more about the way we try to find meaning in our lives but can still be deceived by our senses?

Many people throughout history have believed that humans have not only a physical body but also a separate spiritual body that can live on after death.

Ancient Specters

Belief in an afterlife seems to have existed for centuries. Prehistoric cave paintings may have been attempts by early humans to communicate with their dead ancestors. The ancient Egyptians believed that a person's soul left the body at death, only to be reunited after a proper burial. Let's take a look at two early ghost stories from our past. . . .

A Greek Haunting

One early account of a spectral encounter was recorded by the Greek philosopher Athenodorus, who lived during the 1st century BCE. Against the advice of his friends, the philosopher rented a house that was reputed to be haunted. At night while Athenodorus was writing, the gaunt-faced spirit of an old man in soiled robes appeared. The ghost was weighed down by chains and seemed to be in anguish.

The specter gestured at Athenodorus to follow him and led the philosopher into a courtyard of the house. Athenodorus watched as the ghost appeared to melt into the ground. The next morning, Athenodorus sought the help of local authorities who began to dig at the spot where the ghost had disappeared. There, they unearthed an old skeleton wrapped in rusted chains. The body was then removed and given a proper burial, after which the house was never again troubled by ghosts.

Am I Beautiful?

One of the most frightening of ancient ghost stories comes from Japan, dating perhaps to hundreds of years ago. According to the legend, Kuchisake-onna is a spirit that appears as a woman with long hands, black hair, and pale skin. Her face is covered by a mask or a fan, and she is carrying long scissors or a sharp knife. Kuchisake-onna seeks out solitary young men and women to ask them a simple question: "Am I beautiful?"

If the victim answers "no," then Kuchisake-onna is said to kill them. If they answer "yes," the spirit removes the face covering to reveal a deep cut across her mouth from ear to ear. She then asks, "Am I beautiful now?" If the frightened person screams or answers "no," she kills them. But if they answer "yes," she will try to cut the person across the face. Some stories say that victims can avoid death only by telling the ghost it is of average appearance or by not answering at all and saying they are in a hurry. Others say that a person must distract the spirit in order to escape, throwing candy or money in its direction.

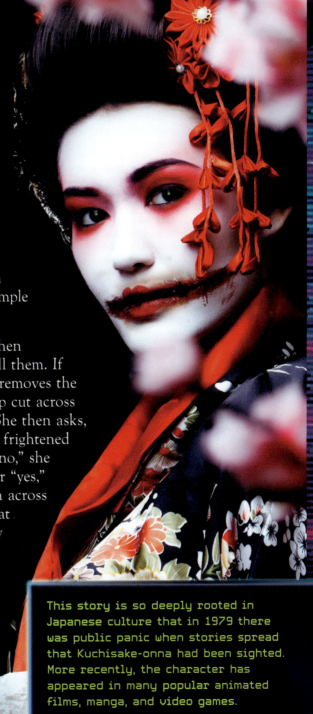

This story is so deeply rooted in Japanese culture that in 1979 there was public panic when stories spread that Kuchisake-onna had been sighted. More recently, the character has appeared in many popular animated films, manga, and video games.

Double (Spirit) Trouble

Most people are familiar with the concept of ghosts—spirits of the deceased that continue to appear after death. But some people believe that even a living person can have a spirit double, making it seem that the person is in two places at once. This apparent bilocation is said to sometimes be a warning of approaching danger or to happen during a near-death experience.

The Absent MP

In 1905, Sir Frederick Carne Rasch was a member of the British Parliament, or an MP. He was known as a hardworking politician who cared about the causes he represented. During preparations for an important vote, Rasch fell ill with influenza and was confined to bed at home. Apparently, this didn't stop him from wanting to be at work at the House of Commons at the very same time.

As the many MPs were preparing for the debate before the vote, several saw Rasch sitting in his usual seat. He appeared stony-faced and pale. His fellow MP Sir Gilbert Parker knew he had been ill and was surprised to see him, saying, "I hope you are better." Rasch made no sign or reply. Parker recalled, "then I turned again towards Sir Carne, and he had vanished. That puzzled me, and I at once went in search of him." But Rasch could not be found. Later, it was confirmed that Sir Carne Rasch was at home the entire time, still too ill to leave. When he returned to Parliament a few days later, other MPs delighted in prodding him to see if he really was there in the flesh.

Many ancient cultures have stories of phantom doubles, where the spirit of a living person can free itself from the body and exist separately from it. The ancient Egyptians called these spirits *ka*, and they were said to possess the same feelings and memories as the person. In German folklore, *doppelgängers* are doubles of living people and usually represent evil. In Norse mythology, a *vardoger* is a ghostly double who is seen performing a person's actions in advance of their arrival.

Getting Ahead of Themselves

Reverend W. Mountford was a well-known English clergyman and author who lived in Boston in the mid 1800s. One day, the reverend was visiting a friend when he looked out the dining room window and saw a carriage approaching. He told his friend that guests were arriving, and the friend joined him at the window where they saw the friend's brother and sister-in-law riding in a carriage on the nearby road. The men watched the carriage pass in front of the house. Rev. Mountford and his friend expected to hear a knock at the front door, but when none came, they went to open it. There was no carriage to be seen.

Several minutes later, the friend's niece arrived at the house and informed them that she had come on foot and that her parents had passed her on the road in their carriage but hadn't stopped or spoken to her. The niece seemed confused. About 10 minutes later, another carriage arrived with the couple. They denied having passed by their daughter and swore to the others that they hadn't yet been to the house. The reverend and his friends were unable to explain the appearance and disappearance of the mysterious phantom carriage.

Reverend Mountford had traveled with his wife to Europe and stayed a long time in Rome, Italy, where he acquired a deep interest in the supernatural. When he returned to Boston, he preached and wrote a great deal about miraculous events and the spiritualism of the time. Perhaps this helped prepare him for spirit doubles that he witnessed the day he visited his friend.

The Mysterious Ms. Sagée

In 1845, Ms. Émilie Sagée began a new job as a teacher at a girls' boarding school called Pennsionat of Neuwelcke, in a region of present-day Latvia. Ms. Sagée was considered skilled at her profession and able to teach at the high standards of the school. She was well-liked by the 42 students, all young girls from wealthy families.

A few weeks after her arrival at the school, strange rumors began to circulate. Some students would claim to have seen the teacher in one part of the school, while others would say they saw her elsewhere at the same time. One day, Ms. Sagée was teaching a class of 13 students and writing on the blackboard. To the amazement of the students, a second Ms. Sagée appeared next to the first, moving with the exact same writing gestures. On another day, the teacher was helping one of the students with her dress. When the student turned to look into the mirror, she saw two versions of Ms. Sagée standing by her. The student fainted from shock.

The stories of Ms. Sagée continued, sometimes with the double close by and imitating the teacher's movements and other times in a different location. One of the most shocking stories took place in front of all 42 students gathered in one room for a lesson. That day, the headmistress was supervising the students and Ms. Sagée was busily gathering flowers just outside the window where they could see her. When the headmistress stepped out of the room for a moment, Ms. Sagée suddenly appeared sitting in the headmistress's chair. The students could also still see their teacher outside, but she now seemed to be moving slowly and with little energy. The Ms. Sagée in the classroom was still and lifeless.

Two brave students decided to approach the classroom version of their teacher. One claimed touching the spirit was like touching soft cloth. The other said she had been able to move completely through part of the phantom. At last, the classroom Ms. Sagée gradually disappeared, and the teacher outside resumed her work in a lively manner. When later asked about the incident, Ms. Sagée said when she saw the headmistress leave the classroom, her only thought was that she wished she could have been in there to watch over her students.

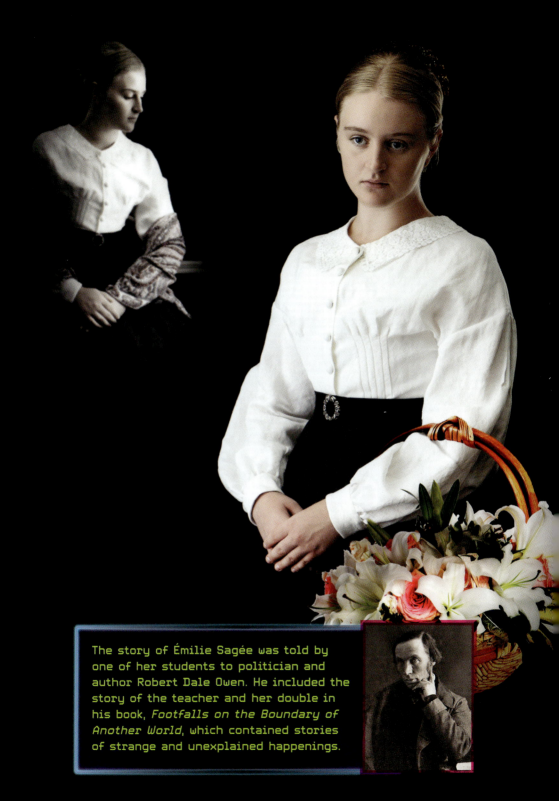

The story of Émilie Sagée was told by one of her students to politician and author Robert Dale Owen. He included the story of the teacher and her double in his book, *Footfalls on the Boundary of Another World*, which contained stories of strange and unexplained happenings.

Steer to the Nor'west!

Robert Bruce was the first mate aboard a cargo ship cutting through the icy waters off the coast of Canada in 1828. After making navigational observations on the deck with the captain, Bruce went down to his cabin belowdecks to check his calculations. He was having difficulty with the math. After working a bit longer, Bruce thought he saw the captain sitting at his desk nearby. When he looked more closely, he realized instead it was a stranger writing on the captain's slate. The figure had an otherworldly appearance and a grave expression. When the stranger raised his head and looked up, Bruce raced away in search of the captain.

Bruce soon found the captain on deck and explained to him what he had seen. He convinced the captain to return with him to the cabin. "I never was a believer in ghosts," said Bruce as they made their way belowdeck, "but if the truth must be told sir, I'd rather not face it alone." When the men entered the cabin, it was empty. They did, however, find the slate, and on it were written the words "Steer to the nor'west."

There are ghostly stories of other ships, too. In 1794, the USS *Constellation* was launched as part of the newly formed United States Navy. Over the many years of its service, the ship was said to be haunted by the ghost of a disgraced sailor, the captain who ordered his death, a ship watchman, and even an 11-year-old boy who died aboard.

To be certain that the mysterious stranger wasn't simply one of the other sailors, the captain instructed all those who were literate to write out the same words that had been found. None of the writing samples matched the one on the slate. Concerned that there was a stowaway, the crew searched the ship everywhere, but no one was found. The captain and his first mate didn't know what to think.

Finally, Bruce and the captain decided to follow the mysterious message and ordered the ship to change course and head northwest. Soon, a sailor keeping watch reported an iceberg ahead. As they approached, they also discovered a ship that had struck the berg and was frozen in the ice. They could see people aboard the wreck, and Bruce quickly ordered boats to be sent to the frozen ship and retrieve the survivors. The ship had been stuck for several weeks, and the passengers had almost run out of food and water. They had nearly lost hope.

Bruce watched as the survivors were brought aboard, one by one. Suddenly, he was startled to see a familiar face—the man he had seen in the cabin who had written the message! After the survivor had sufficiently recovered, Bruce and the captain asked him to copy the message on the slate. The two sets of handwriting were identical. Initially, the stranger couldn't account for his presence on the ship, until he recalled a dream that he had had about the same time that Bruce had seen his ghost at the captain's desk.

The stranger said that after falling asleep from exhaustion, he had dreamed that he was aboard a ship that was coming to rescue him and his fellow survivors. When he woke, he told the captain of his own ship and the other passengers about his dream. He assured them that help was on its way, and he even described the ship that was coming to rescue them. The captain of the wrecked ship confirmed his story. "He described her appearance and rig," he told their rescuers. "And, to our utter astonishment, when your vessel hove in sight, she corresponded exactly to his description of her."

> The man who first recounted this story was Captain J. S. Clarke, a friend of Robert Bruce. The two men were close and had sailed together for more than a year. When asked about the honesty of Bruce, Capt. Clarke replied that he was "as truthful and straightforward a man as ever I met in all my life. . . . I'd stake my life upon it that he told me no lie."

Near to Death

Ghosts are said to be the essence of people after their death. But what about when a person doesn't quite die? For decades, near-death experiences have been reported by people who have been thought to be clinically dead but later have regained consciousness. Although no two reports of the experiences are the same, they tend to share some things in common.

Many people claim in near-death experiences that they feel as if they have risen out of their bodies. They look down at themselves surrounded by medical teams trying to bring their bodies back to life. Some people can recall exactly what happened in the room where they lay, including details such as what was spoken by doctors and nurses or which instruments were used.

Other people report experiences at the time of their death that involve hovering above members of their family. Some say that seeing their loved ones became the reason they returned to their bodies. Many describe a feeling of peace and joy that swept over them or say that they found themselves in a dark tunnel with a beautiful white or golden light at the end. Sometimes, people claim to have heard the voices of deceased loved ones urging them to return to Earth to stay among the living.

In 2001, *The Lancet* medical journal published a 13-year study on near-death experiences in Dutch hospitals. The investigation was conducted by cardiologist Pim van Lommel and involved interviewing 344 patients immediately after they had been resuscitated. Twelve percent of the patients reported having a deep experience—ones involving leaving the body, seeing a bright light, or meeting dead relatives. Interestingly, the details of their experiences remained the same, even when they were questioned again two and eight years later. The study also noted that those who had near-death experiences seemed to have a much greater appreciation for life and much less fear of death.

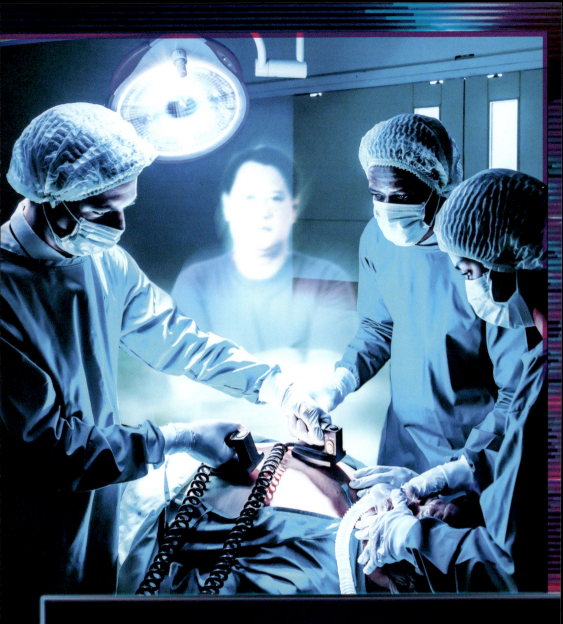

In 1889, Dr. A. S. Wiltse of Skiddy, Kansas, contracted typhoid fever and lapsed into unconsciousness. He wrote of his near-death experience in the *St. Louis Medical Review and Surgical Journal*.

I came again into a state of conscious existence and discovered that I was still in the body, but the body and I had no interests in common. I had died. . . . I watched the interesting process of the separation of the soul from the body. . . . I saw a number of persons sitting and standing about the body. . . . I bowed to them playfully and saluted with my right hand. . . . The situation struck me as humorous, and I laughed outright.

Talking to the Dead

While many people claim to have seen ghosts, others say they simply wish to speak with the dead. After a person dies, family members, friends, and other loved ones sometimes seek out mediums, or people said to possess the ability to communicate with the dead. The mediums often claim to have an awareness of the world beyond the five senses that allows them to hear, see, and otherwise sense spirits around us.

He Hasn't Left

English medium Jill Nash sees her role as one of helping the bereaved attain closure. She claims to help facilitate a reunion between the living and the dead, giving them another chance to see one another. Nash describes one occasion when a woman visited her to attempt to contact her husband, who had recently died. The woman apparently wasn't alone. Nash states,

> I opened the door expecting to see a little elderly lady and instead saw her and her late husband. He walked in behind her. She was, of course, unaware that he was with her, but I could see him plain as day, although he was fainter than a living person, almost transparent, and there was nothing to see below the knee. He was tall and slim and when she sat down, he stood behind her with a satisfied grin on his face as if he was thinking, "At last, now I can tell her what I have been trying to say to her for months." He asked me to tell her that he often stood behind her, and that if she felt something brushing against her cheek or a gentle pat on the head that it was only him reassuring her that he was still around. And as soon as I said that she admitted that she had felt these things and had wondered if it was him.

Mediums are a type of psychic, a person who claims to have the ability to sense nonphysical and supernatural forces or to have mysterious perceptions or understandings. All kinds of paranormal powers are attributed to psychics, including precognition, or the ability to foresee the future, and remote viewing, or being capable of projecting one's consciousness to another location.

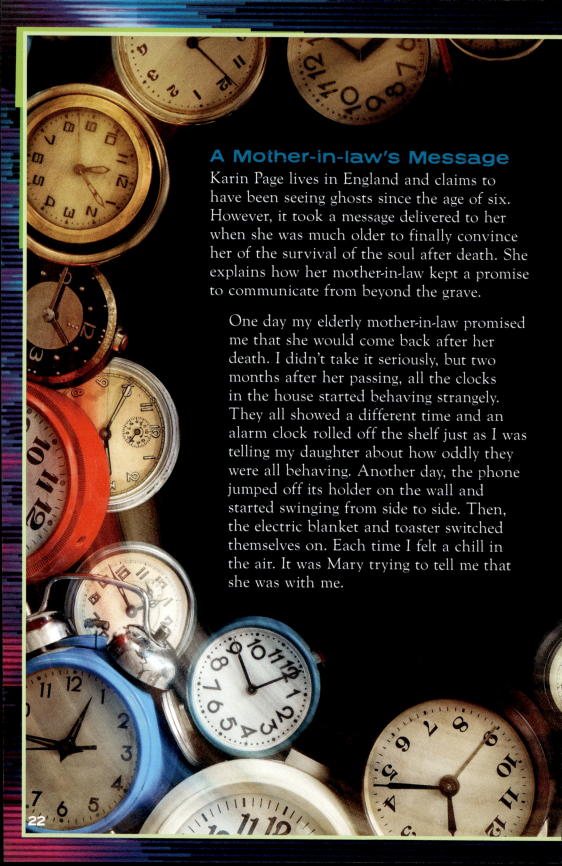

A Mother-in-law's Message

Karin Page lives in England and claims to have been seeing ghosts since the age of six. However, it took a message delivered to her when she was much older to finally convince her of the survival of the soul after death. She explains how her mother-in-law kept a promise to communicate from beyond the grave.

One day my elderly mother-in-law promised me that she would come back after her death. I didn't take it seriously, but two months after her passing, all the clocks in the house started behaving strangely. They all showed a different time and an alarm clock rolled off the shelf just as I was telling my daughter about how oddly they were all behaving. Another day, the phone jumped off its holder on the wall and started swinging from side to side. Then, the electric blanket and toaster switched themselves on. Each time I felt a chill in the air. It was Mary trying to tell me that she was with me.

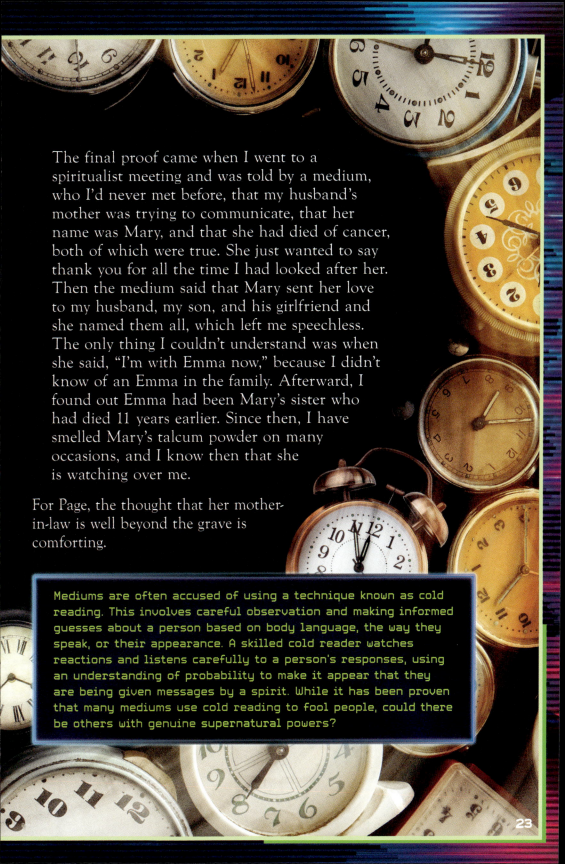

The final proof came when I went to a spiritualist meeting and was told by a medium, who I'd never met before, that my husband's mother was trying to communicate, that her name was Mary, and that she had died of cancer, both of which were true. She just wanted to say thank you for all the time I had looked after her. Then the medium said that Mary sent her love to my husband, my son, and his girlfriend and she named them all, which left me speechless. The only thing I couldn't understand was when she said, "I'm with Emma now," because I didn't know of an Emma in the family. Afterward, I found out Emma had been Mary's sister who had died 11 years earlier. Since then, I have smelled Mary's talcum powder on many occasions, and I know then that she is watching over me.

For Page, the thought that her mother-in-law is well beyond the grave is comforting.

> Mediums are often accused of using a technique known as cold reading. This involves careful observation and making informed guesses about a person based on body language, the way they speak, or their appearance. A skilled cold reader watches reactions and listens carefully to a person's responses, using an understanding of probability to make it appear that they are being given messages by a spirit. While it has been proven that many mediums use cold reading to fool people, could there be others with genuine supernatural powers?

The Vennum Case

Late in the summer of 1877, Mary Lurancy Vennum, a 13-year-old girl from Watseka, Illinois, told her family something extraordinary. She said, "There were persons in my room last night, and they called 'Rancy! Rancy!'" using her nickname. The next day, Lurancy suffered a series of convulsions, falling into a trancelike state for hours at a time. While her body was rigid in this state, she spoke freely of seeing spirits, including a brother and sister of hers who had died some years earlier.

The trances and violent fits continued for months, sometimes as often as 12 times a day. Some people were afraid Lurancy had lost her mind, while others believed evil spirits had possessed the girl. The family was ready to place Lurancy in an asylum when a neighbor, Asa Roff, convinced them to first see the doctor and spiritualist E. Winchester Stevens. At the end of January 1878, Mr. Roff brought Dr. Stevens to visit the Vennum house.

When Dr. Stevens met Lurancy, she sat with her elbows on her knees, her hands under her chin, and her feet curled under the chair. She spoke to Dr. Stevens in the voice of an old woman and said her name was Katrina Hogan, a 63-year-old grandmother from Germany. Soon, Lurancy's personality changed to a man named Willie, and she provided details about his life. The changes continued, with Lurancy sometimes switching suddenly from quiet sadness to joyous descriptions of visits with angels. Several other voices and personalities came through her as well, although Lurancy would seemingly return to herself from time to time to say that evil spirits had been controlling her.

> Possession has been described as a spirit, a demon, or some other entity taking control of a human body, often changing the health, emotions, and personality of the victim. Today, psychologists and other health professionals are often able to treat patients with similar symptoms using a combination of medication and modern therapy practices.

Lurancy soon spoke of another spirit wanting to come through, saying aloud the name of Mary Roff. The neighbor was shocked. "That is my daughter," he exclaimed. "Mary Roff is my girl. Why, she has been in heaven 12 years." Lurancy continued to talk and seemed to be speaking with the voice of Mary Roff. She spoke about how much she missed her family. Dr. Stevens later wrote that this was "the most remarkable case of spirit return and manifestation ever recorded in history."

For the next week or so, the personality of Mary Roff was the only one to come through Lurancy. The fits had stopped, and Lurancy appeared calm, mild, and polite. Mrs. Roff and her adult daughter wanted to visit and see for themselves the girl who seemed to have the spirit of Mary inside her. As the mother and daughter approached the house, Lurancy exclaimed, "There comes my ma and sister Nervie!" using the name that Mary Roff had called her sister many years before. She rushed up, hugged them, and seemed very happy to see them.

The personality of Mary Roff seemed to become more and more homesick as time went on, and the voice coming from Lurancy begged to return to her home. Finally, on February 11, the Vennum family agreed to allow Lurancy to stay awhile with the Roffs, hoping that she would improve. When she arrived at the Roff home, she greeted each member of the family warmly, as if she knew them all. She appeared perfectly happy and content to be in their home and seemed to remember many events of Mary Roff's life, even recognizing friends and neighbors from years before. Even more strangely, Lurancy soon appeared unable to recognize her parents, Mr. and Mrs. Vennum, when they came to visit.

Mr. Roff wrote of the new arrival into their family.

> You know how we took the poor, dear girl Lurancy (Mary). Some appreciate our motives, but the many, without investigation and without a knowledge of the facts, cry out against us and against that angel girl. Some say she pretends; others that she is crazy; and we hear that some say it is the devil. Mary is perfectly happy; she recognizes everybody and everything she knew when in her body 12 or more years ago.

Lurancy stayed with the Roffs for several weeks. Eventually, the spirit of Mary would seem to leave for short periods, with Lurancy returning to her previous self. She claimed the spirit of Mary was getting ready to leave, soon allowing Lurancy full control over her body. Lurancy returned to the Vennum house where she stayed until she left to be married and begin a family of her own.

Lurancy Vennum

Mary Roff

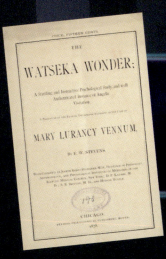

Dr. E. Winchester Stevens described the strange story of Lurancy Vennum in his book *The Watseka Wonder: Startling and Instructive Psychological Study, and Well Authenticated Instance of Angelic Visitation*. He published his work in 1887.

Did the Sisters Return?

In 1957 in Hexham, England, tragedy struck John and Florence Pollock. A car had swerved off the road and hit their two daughters, Joanna, 11 years old, and Jacqueline, 6 years old, while the children were walking to church with a friend. The girls were killed instantly.

The parents were devastated. Florence was so upset that she tried not to think about their daughters at all. John, on the other hand, seemed to think of nothing else. He claimed he had had a vision on the night of the girls' deaths, seeing them in heaven. John had long believed in reincarnation and became convinced that the spirits of his daughters would return to the family, reborn as different children.

Soon, Florence became pregnant, and John predicted that the couple would have twins. Florence disagreed; neither of their families had a history of twins, and her doctor had indicated she would have only one baby. However, John was right. In October 1958, Florence gave birth to identical twin girls, and the couple named them Gillian and Jennifer. About 9 months later, the family moved to a town about 30 miles (50 km) away from Hexham.

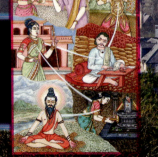

Reincarnation is the belief that the spirit of a person comes back to life in a new form following the death of the body. It is an important part of Hinduism, Buddhism, Jainism, and Sikhism, as well as other religions.

Despite being identical twins, the girls had some unusual physical differences. Jennifer was born with a thin birthmark on her forehead that matched the shape of a scar on the forehead of her dead sister Jacqueline. Even stranger, both Jennifer and Jacqueline had brown, thumbprint-shaped birthmarks in the same place on their left hips. As the babies learned to walk, the parents were surprised to see Gillian walk with her feet pointing slightly outward, just as her sister Joanna had done. Jennifer walked in a more straightforward way, like Jacqueline.

When the girls were about three and a half years old, their father took them back to Hexham for the first time. He claimed that Gillian and Jennifer pointed out places they had never seen and talked about where they had played. He said the twins knew when they were approaching their school, although the place where their older sisters had attended was not yet within sight. The girls were also able to identify their former house as they passed it despite their father having said nothing about it.

Hexham, England

Gillian and Jennifer Pollock sit with a researcher while their father, John Pollock, stands behind them.

About six months later, the twins were given a box with toys that had belonged to their sisters. Gillian picked up Joanna's toys, and Jennifer chose Jacqueline's, as if they were familiar with them. They even knew which had been given as Christmas gifts. The girls picked up two dolls and claimed one was named Mary and the other Susan. Their mother was astonished; those had been the very names that Joanna and Jacqueline had given the dolls.

Although their parents hadn't talked about their older daughters' accident in front of the twins, they occasionally overheard the young girls discussing the details of it. In addition, Florence said she once saw the twins playing a game she found disturbing. Jennifer was lying on the floor acting as if she were dying, with her head in Gillian's lap. Gillian said to her sister, "The blood's coming out of your eyes. That's where the car hit you."

Both Gillian and Jennifer had a phobia related to cars and often had nightmares about them. Florence noticed that the twins would be especially careful crossing streets and would hold tightly on to her hands. On one occasion, the mother said she heard the girls screaming outside the house. When she came out, she saw them clutching each other and looking terrified in the direction of a stationary car with its motor running. The girls were crying, "The car! It's coming at us!"

At about five years old, the strange instances that recalled a previous life began to diminish. Gillian and Jennifer grew into normal, healthy children and then into well-adjusted adults.

Ian Stevenson was a psychiatrist who was convinced that reincarnation could account for emotions, memories, and even physical characteristics that could not be fully explained by genetics or the environment alone. Over a period of 40 years, Stevenson investigated 2,500 reports of young children who claimed to remember a past life. He compared the children's statements with any facts he could find about the deceased person they identified. He also matched birthmarks and birth defects to wounds and scars on the deceased. He wrote 14 books and hundreds of scientific papers on the topic of reincarnation.

The Bloody Tower

The Tower of London is a historic castle on the north side of the River Thames in London, England. Throughout British history, the Tower has served many purposes, including a royal residence, a treasury, and a public records office. It has also been a notorious prison and the site of many executions. It's no wonder, then, that the Tower has a reputation for spectral sightings.

For hundreds of years, at least six ravens have been kept at the Tower of London. There is a legend that says if the ravens ever leave, the Tower will fall.

Ghost Brothers

Among the Tower's most famous residents were the young princes Edward and Richard, who were imprisoned in the tower in 1483 by their uncle, the Duke of Gloucester. It is believed that the duke ordered the murder of his nephews so he could be crowned King Richard III. Ghosts of the princes have been sighted several times, walking hand in hand through the stone corridors of the Tower, perhaps searching for their murderous uncle.

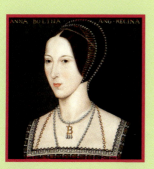

Headless!

Anne Boleyn was the second wife of King Henry VIII, who was made prisoner and then later beheaded at the Tower in 1536. Some 340 years later, a soldier reported seeing a light in the chapel. When he climbed to a window to look in, he reported seeing a ghostly procession of knights and ladies, led by a headless Anne Boleyn.

The Executioner's Pursuit

Margaret Pole, Countess of Salisbury, was 67 years old in 1541 when she was condemned to death by Henry VIII. At her execution, Pole refused to kneel but instead commanded her executioner to cut off her head as she stood. When he refused, Pole fled, forcing him to pursue her swinging his weapon. It is said that at night on the anniversary of her execution, the ghosts of Pole and her executioner reenact the bloody scene.

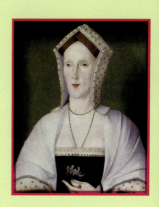

The Nine Days Queen

At only 15, Lady Jane Grey became queen after the death of King Edward VI. The young queen ruled for just nine days before she was arrested and sentenced to death in February 1554. Many witnesses have since seen her grieving ghost. In 1957, two sentries swore they saw an apparition of the young queen change into a ball of light on one of the battlements of the Tower.

Lincoln's Ghost

In April 1865, President Abraham Lincoln had a dream. In it, he described walking through the White House and coming upon a wrapped corpse with soldiers standing guard and crowds of people weeping and staring at the body. In the dream Lincoln asked a guard who had died, and the guard responded, "The president. He was killed by an assassin." Three days later, President Lincoln was shot to death by John Wilkes Booth.

Since his tragic death, the ghost of Abraham Lincoln has been seen several times at the White House. In 1927, First Lady Grace Coolidge said she saw a phantom Lincoln in the Yellow Oval Room, staring blankly out of a window. Queen Wilhelmina of the Netherlands visited President Franklin and Mrs. Roosevelt in 1942. While in her bedroom at night, she heard a knock on the door. When she answered, she saw the ghost of Lincoln standing before her in a long coat and top hat. She promptly fainted. In the late 1940s, President Harry Truman and his daughter, Margaret Truman, both reportedly heard knocking coming from the Lincoln bedroom on several occasions.

During World War II (1939–1945), British Prime Minister Winston Churchill visited the Roosevelts at the White House. It is said that the prime minister enjoyed hot baths at the end of the day. One evening, Churchill claimed he was getting out of his bath and went to look for a towel when he noticed a man standing by the fireplace. It was the ghost of Abraham Lincoln. According to a newspaper at the time, the prime minister said, "Good evening, Mr. President. You seem to have me at a disadvantage." The ghost is said to have smiled and then faded away.

The president was not the only Lincoln ghost people claim to have seen at the White House. In 1862, William Wallace "Willie" Lincoln, the president's son, died of typhoid when he was just 11 years old. Willie's ghost was first seen in the White House when Ulysses S. Grant was president in the 1870s. Since then, the phantom has been seen several times, including by the daughter of President Lyndon B. Johnson in the 1960s.

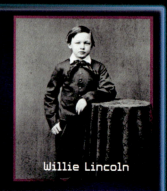

Willie Lincoln

Did President Lincoln visit the Yellow Oval Room after his death?

Ghosts of Alcatraz

Alcatraz, the small, rocky island in the San Francisco Bay, has a long history. In the 1800s, the island was developed and used as a lighthouse, a fortress, and a military prison. In 1934, it was converted into a maximum-security federal prison where escape was considered nearly impossible because of the harsh conditions in the water swirling around the island. In 1963, the prison closed, and the island soon became a popular tourist attraction.

Over the years, many have reported supernatural happenings in the prison. Several inmates were said to have been driven mentally ill by mysterious sightings and constant noises in the night. Guards would sometimes hear desperate sobbing or moaning, encounter terrible smells, or see phantom soldiers and prisoners. During foggy nights, some claimed to have seen an old lighthouse appear on the island, accompanied by a whistle and flashing green lights, all of which would soon fade away.

Perhaps one of the eeriest stories is said to have happened in D-block, a group of six small cells, collectively known as the Hole, that were intended to house the worst prisoners. In the 1940s, one prisoner was put into a cell in the Hole, and he immediately began to scream that something with glowing eyes was inside the cell with him. The guards ignored him, and the following morning, the prisoner was found dead with bruises on his neck. An autopsy revealed that he died of strangulation, despite having been alone in the cell. The next day, when the guards were counting the other prisoners, there was one extra. When a guard looked more closely, he saw among the prisoners the man who had died the previous night. The apparition quickly vanished.

Since Alcatraz has opened to tourists, some visitors claim to have seen cell doors closing by themselves and to have heard phantom footsteps, the screams of prisoners, and other cries of agony. Others have reported seeing phantom inmates pass along the corridors and out through solid walls. Many visitors to Alcatraz have had the eerie feeling of being watched even though nearby corridors and cells were empty.

Infamous gangster and mob boss Al Capone was brought to Alcatraz in 1934. Surprisingly, Capone was a model inmate and was allowed to play the banjo in the prison band. Recent tour guides and visitors to the island have reported hearing ghostly banjo music coming from the cell where Capone stayed.

A Poet's Haunted House

Edgar Allan Poe is an American author best known for his poems and short stories, many of which are considered Gothic horror due to their dark themes. As a young man in the 1830s, Poe lived in a narrow brick house on North Amity Street in Baltimore, Maryland. Today, the house is a museum and is said to be haunted by more than just the writer's eerie stories.

In 1968, the police were called to the Poe house to investigate a possible burglary. When they arrived, they claimed to see a light inside the house through the ground floor window. The light then floated up and reappeared on the second floor, before moving up to the attic where the poet used to work. When the police entered the property, the house was empty and there was no one to be seen. They never found the source of the light.

Many other spooky incidents are connected to the house. The sad gaze from an eerie portrait of Poe's wife seems to follow visitors around the room. Neighbors have reported seeing a shadowy figure through a second-floor window. Museum workers have recorded many incidents of supernatural activity that seem to originate in the bedroom that belonged to Poe's grandmother. Doors and windows have mysteriously opened and closed, and visitors have reported feeling someone tap them on the shoulder when no one is there. Psychic investigators who have visited the house even claim to have seen the ghost of a silvery-haired old woman gliding through the rooms.

One of Poe's most well-known works is the narrative poem "The Raven." The supernatural tale tells of a man mourning the loss of his love, Lenore, when he is visited at midnight by a talking raven. The mysterious bird repeatedly answers the man's questions with a single word, "Nevermore," causing him to fall into even more sadness. The famous poem makes use of folklore, religion, and history to captivate its readers.

The Poe house on North Amity Street

Spirits "R" Us

In 1970, when a new Toys "R" Us store was built in Sunnyvale, California, nobody expected it to become famous for having a ghost. But soon after the store was opened, employees began to report strange occurrences.

In the morning, workers would arrive to find toys scattered across the floor or items moved to the wrong shelves. Some claimed to have seen dolls fly off the shelves and balls mysteriously fall and bounce down the aisles. Others said they smelled fresh flowers or felt a cold breeze on their backs. Still others heard disembodied voices call their names or felt an invisible hand touch them. Soon, employees began to quit.

As the unusual reports continued, the toy store gathered more and more attention. Soon, local psychic Sylvia Brown decided to spend the night and hold a séance, hoping to discover the source of the haunting. After the workers had left, Brown, along with a photographer and other guests, began to attempt to contact any unseen spirits.

According to Brown, she sensed a tall, thin man walking down the aisle toward her. She said he spoke with a Swedish accent and identified himself as a preacher named Johnny Johnson. The ghost said he had worked on the land the store had been built upon when it was John Murphy's farm in the 1880s. Johnson had fallen in love with Murphy's daughter, but she left him for another man. Tragically, Johnson injured himself chopping trees and, unable to go get help, he bled to death.

After several more séances, Brown said she was also able to discover that the ghost found the toy store and its visitors annoying and loud. Perhaps it was the noisy crowds combined with the sadness of a lost love that made Johnny Johnson cause so much toy trouble.

The reality TV show *That's Incredible* from the early 1980s featured scientific or medical breakthroughs, people with unusual talents, stunt performances, and reenactments of allegedly paranormal events. In an episode featuring the Sunnyvale Toys "R" Us, the show used actors to show what might have happened during one of Brown's séances. Afterward, the psychic and the toy store became world-famous.

Sylvia Brown

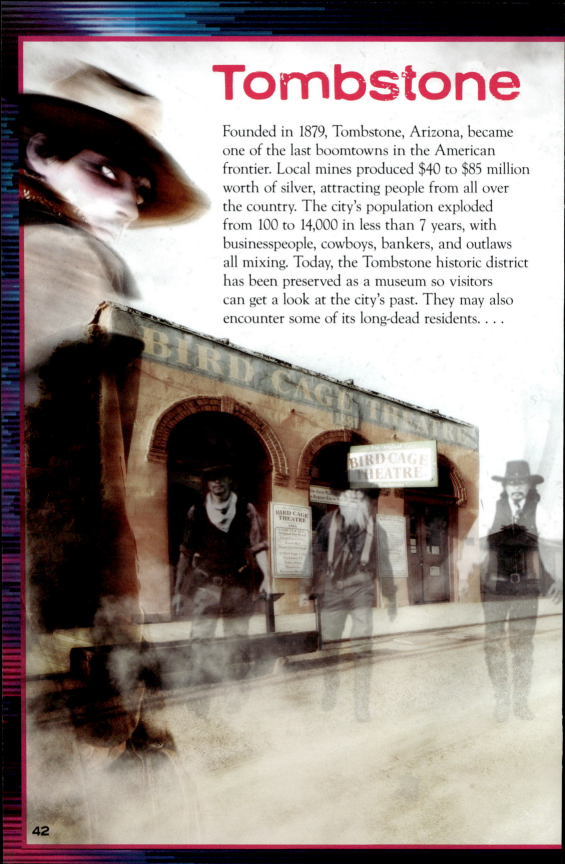

Tombstone

Founded in 1879, Tombstone, Arizona, became one of the last boomtowns in the American frontier. Local mines produced $40 to $85 million worth of silver, attracting people from all over the country. The city's population exploded from 100 to 14,000 in less than 7 years, with businesspeople, cowboys, bankers, and outlaws all mixing. Today, the Tombstone historic district has been preserved as a museum so visitors can get a look at the city's past. They may also encounter some of its long-dead residents. . . .

Local tour guides often tell visitors that as many as 31 ghosts are thought to haunt the Bird Cage Theatre saloon, one of the city's oldest buildings and the site of 26 killings. Many people have sighted apparitions dressed in clothing from the 1800s. The phantom most frequently seen in the saloon is a stagehand wearing black striped trousers and carrying a clipboard. He is said to appear from nowhere, walk across the stage, and exit through a solid wall. Some visitors have heard the faint sounds of a woman singing, old-time music suddenly playing, or the noises of glasses clinking and cards shuffling when no one is around.

There have been other mysterious goings-on as well. Visitors have sometimes remarked on the strong smell of cigar smoke near the card tables, although smoking is prohibited on the site. Staff members claim that furniture has moved by itself and one tour guide was apparently struck on the back of the knee, causing him to fall to the floor. When he looked around, he said there was no one in sight. One strange story involves a $100 poker chip that is said to have appeared on the poker table one day. After a worker had locked it away in a desk, it soon vanished and turned up in a filing cabinet some days later. Perhaps the town's busy history has led to this equally busy afterlife.

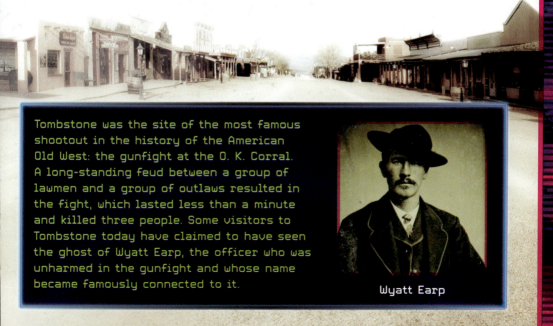

Tombstone was the site of the most famous shootout in the history of the American Old West: the gunfight at the O. K. Corral. A long-standing feud between a group of lawmen and a group of outlaws resulted in the fight, which lasted less than a minute and killed three people. Some visitors to Tombstone today have claimed to have seen the ghost of Wyatt Earp, the officer who was unharmed in the gunfight and whose name became famously connected to it.

Wyatt Earp

Glossary

apparition a ghost or ghostlike image

assassin a person who kills a politically important person

authenticated proved to be true or genuine

autopsy a postmortem examination to discover the cause of death

bereaved suffering the death of a loved one

bilocation the phenomenon of appearing in two places at once

boomtowns towns experiencing a sudden growth in business and population

Buddhism an Asian religion or philosophy founded by Siddhartha Gautama in north-eastern India in the 5th century BCE

cardiologist a doctor who studies the heart and its health

cargo a load of goods or supplies

condemned pronounced guilty and sentenced to punishment

consciousness the state of being awake and aware

convulsions uncontrollable movements of the body

deceased no longer living

disgraced having brought shame or dishonor

essence the basic nature of a thing that make it what it is

evidence objects or information that can be used to prove whether something is true

executions acts of killing someone as punishment for a crime

facilitate to make something easier

feud a bitter argument between two people or groups that lasts for a long time

gaunt thin and bony

genetics biological characteristics, traits, or tendencies that are passed down to children from their parents

gestures motions of the limbs or body to express something

headmistress a female teacher who is in charge of a school

hovering floating in place in the air

investigation a search to find out the facts or the truth about something

literate able to read and write

mediums people claiming to be in contact with the spirits of the dead and able to communicate between the dead and the living

navigational relating to the act of finding your way from one place to another

near-death experience an event that takes place on the brink of death and that is recounted by a person after recovery

paranormal describing events or phenomena that are beyond the scope of normal scientific understanding

Parliament a group of people who have been elected to make laws in England

phantom a ghost or ghostlike image

phobia an extreme fear of something

possession the state of being controlled by a demon or spirit

precognition foreknowledge of an event, especially of a paranormal kind

probability the chance that an event will occur

procession a group of individuals moving along in an orderly, often ceremonial, way

psychic a person considered or claiming to have supernatural powers

reenactments performances of events that happened in the past

reincarnation the rebirth of a soul in a new body

resuscitated revived from unconsciousness or apparent death

séance a meeting at which people attempt to make contact with the dead, especially with the help of a medium

specter a ghost

stowaway a person who hides aboard a ship

strangulation the act of choking someone to death

supernatural something unusual, and often scary, that breaks the laws of nature

trances half-conscious states characterized by an absence of response to external stimuli

transparent able to be seen through

utter to the utmost point or highest degree

witnessed saw something happen

Read More

Allen, Judy and Dinah Williams. *Alarming Afterlife: Scary Cemeteries and Graveyards (Where You Dare Not Go).* Minneapolis: Bearport Publishing Company, 2025.

Finn, Peter. *Do Ghosts Exist? (Fact or Fiction?).* New York: Gareth Stevens Publishing, 2022.

Hansen, Grace. *History's Spookiest Paranormal Events (History's Greatest Mysteries).* Minneapolis: ABDO, 2023.

Sheen, Barbara. *Ghosts and Spirits (Exploring the Occult).* San Diego, CA: ReferencePoint Press, 2024.

Learn More Online

1. Go to **FactSurfer.com** or scan the QR code below.
2. Enter "Phantoms among Us" into the search box.
3. Click on the cover of this book to see a list of websites.

Index

afterlife 6, 43
Alcatraz 36–37
ancient Egypt 6, 9
Boleyn, Anne 33
Brown, Sylvia 40–41
Buddhism 28
Capone, Al 37
Churchill, Winston 34
cold readings 23
Earp, Marshall Wyatt 43
ghost carriages 10–11
Grey, Lady Jane 33
Henry VIII, King 33
Lincoln, President Abraham 34–35
Lommel, Pim van 18
mediums 20, 23
Mountford, Rev. W. 10–11
Nash, Jill 20
Page, Karin 22
past-life memories 31
Poe, Edgar Allan 38–39
Pole, Margaret 33
Pollock family 28, 30
Princes in the Tower 33
psychics 21, 40–41
Rasch, Sir Frederick Carne 8
reincarnation 28, 31
Richard III, King 33
Roff, Mary 24–27
Roosevelt, Franklin D. and Eleanor 34
séances 40–41
spirit doubles 8, 11
Tombstone, Arizona 42–43
Tower of London 32
Toys "R" Us, Sunnyvale 40–41
Vennum, Lurancy 24–27
Wilhelmina, Queen 34